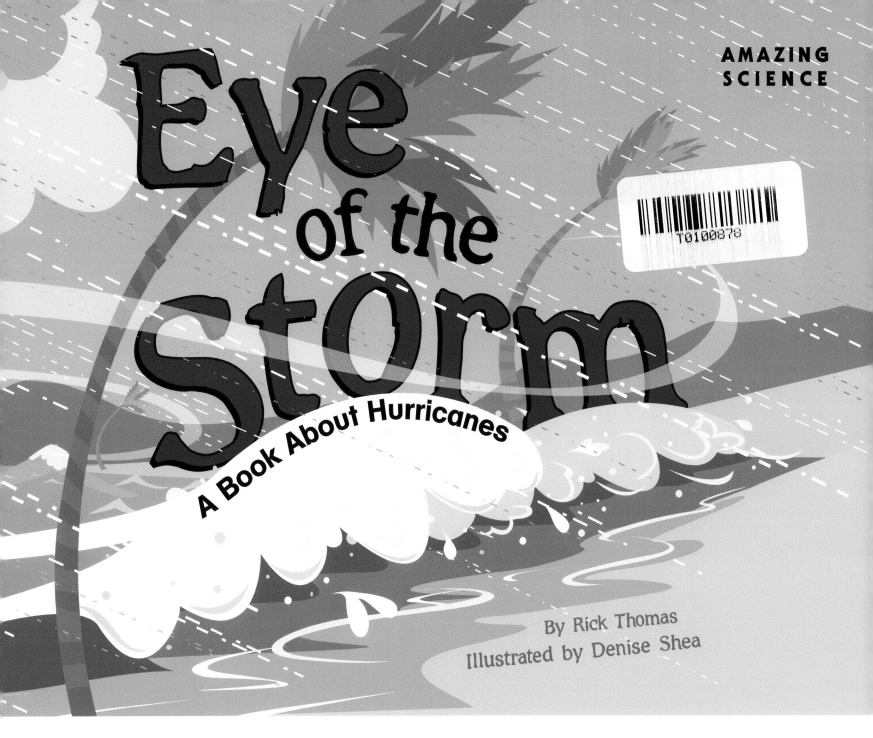

Eye of the Storm

A Book About Hurricanes

By Rick Thomas

Illustrated by Denise Shea

Content Adviser: Daniel Dix, Senior Meteorologist,
The Weather Channel

Reading Adviser: Susan Kesselring, M.A., Literacy Educator,
Rosemount-Apple Valley-Eagan (Minnesota) School District

PICTURE WINDOW BOOKS
Minneapolis, Minnesota

Managing Editor: Catherine Neitge
Creative Director: Terri Foley
Art Director: Keith Griffin
Editor: Patricia Stockland
Designer: Nathan Gassman
Page production: Picture Window Books
The illustrations in this book were prepared digitally.

Picture Window Books
1710 Roe Crest Drive
North Mankato, Minnesota 56003
www.capstonepub.com

Library of Congress Cataloging-in-Publication Data

Thomas, Rick, 1954-
Eye of the storm : a book about hurricanes /
by Rick Thomas ; illustrated by Denise Shea.
p. cm. — (Amazing science)
Includes bibliographical references and index.
ISBN-13: 978-1-4048-0928-4 (hardcover)
ISBN-10: 1-4048-0928-7 (hardcover)
ISBN-13: 978-1-4048-1845-3 (paperback)
ISBN-10: 1-4048-1845-6 (paperback)
1. Hurricanes—Juvenile literature.
I. Shea, Denise, ill. II. Title. III. Series.

QC944.2.T46 2004
551.55'2—dc22
2004019190

Printed in the United States   5442

Table of Contents

A warm, gentle breeze blows. Low waves roll up on the beach. Their foamy white edges splash on the sand. Giant early morning clouds glow pink, red, and gold.

Far, far out on the ocean, a hurricane is growing.

Tropical Storms

Millions of water droplets fill the Atlantic Ocean. Warm, tropical sunlight heats the water. The water rises into the air as vapor.

Rain clouds quickly become tropical thunderstorms. Then the storms drift apart. Tropical storms are the beginning of a hurricane. Hurricanes keep growing. They are fed by warm, spinning air and an endless supply of water from the ocean.

Hurricane!

In the middle of the Atlantic Ocean, small tropical disturbances race above the Equator. The warm air near the Equator rises and dips and moves in circles. When a storm gets caught in the spinning air, it grows larger and stronger.

Dark clouds appear. They are pulled into the storm's twisting winds, like bathwater sucked into a drain. More thunderclouds gather and grow. They crash and cluster together. These thunderclouds form a single, super-sized system of storms. When its winds reach a speed of 74 miles per hour, weather watchers call the storm a hurricane.

Moving Walls of Wind

The sky grows black above the ocean.
The massive group of thunderstorms
flings out a powerful wall of wind.

The storm wind pushes wave after
rushing wave toward faraway shores.
And though a hurricane spins, its
fierce winds blow in one direction.

The hurricane moves slowly away from where it was born. Winds move the hurricane toward land.

Storm Signs

In the sky, the golden clouds have dissolved into one huge curtain of dark gray. The winds begin to blow harder. The waves hit the sand faster. That means the hurricane is closer.

No birds chatter or sing.
They flew away days ago. Growing
breezes warned them of the storm.
Many people flee inland to escape the
hurricane. For people on tropical islands,
it is harder to leave.

Landfall

The next day, the hurricane comes ashore. Once a hurricane makes landfall, or arrives on solid ground, it slows down. There is no deep ocean water below the storm to keep feeding it.

But an island cannot stop a hurricane. Too much water surrounds the small piece of land. Mighty winds whip the trees. High waves race up the shore. The storm rips roofs off houses and tips over cars. Power cables snap. Boats are lifted from the shore and crash inland.

Eye of the Hurricane

A hurricane rages for hours and hours. The storm grows louder and louder. It rains harder and harder.

Suddenly, the angry howling stops. Outside, nothing moves. Straight up in the sky, a patch of stars is surrounded by thick darkness. This is the center of the storm, the eye of the hurricane, as it passes over the land.

The peace and calm will last for only a few minutes. Then the storm will rage as strongly as before. But during the second half of the storm, the winds will come from the opposite direction.

Storm Surge

Both the wind and the water are very damaging. During the storm, rain falls in heavy sheets. Also, the winds shove a huge wall of water onto shore. The wall, called a storm surge, can rise higher than a two-story house. A powerful surge can sweep away cars, buildings, and people.

Once the hurricane has passed, the winds die down. The clouds grow lighter. But the flood and damage remain.

After the Storm

Pale green clouds cover the sky. Throughout the neighborhood, roofs are missing. Trees are tipped over. Wet leaves are plastered onto windows and walls. Streets are covered with water, broken glass, and sputtering, sparking power lines.

But the hurricane is over. The birds are flying back.

Surviving a Hurricane

Most people evacuate, or leave their homes, before a hurricane hits. Not everyone has a place to go or can escape in time. In case you can't leave your home, here are some ways to prepare for a hurricane.

- Tape an X across every window. If the wind breaks them, the tape might help to hold the shattered pieces together.

- Fill up pots, pans, sinks, and bathtubs with water. Hurricanes bring floods that can damage plumbing, knock over water towers, or fill pipes with unhealthy seawater. You need your own supply of water for drinking and washing. If you have pets, remember that they need water, too.

- Inside the house, block windows and doors with heavy furniture, or hammer boards across them.

- Check the batteries in your radio. If power lines are blown away, a small radio will inform you of news about the hurricane.

- Stay inside until the storm blows over. Local police, the National Guard, and the Red Cross will make sure that everyone gets the help they need.

Extreme Storm Extras

- In North and Central America, the official hurricane season lasts from June 1 to November 30, but hurricanes can happen at any time of year.

- Each year, winds and water create about 50 hurricanes.

- Hurricanes are slow-moving storms. Storm trackers can warn endangered communities about a hurricane days before the storm arrives.

- Early warnings save many lives, but the storms are still deadly. In 1995, Hurricane Mitch hit Honduras and Nicaragua, killing more than 10,000 people.

- Names for hurricanes began in 1950 and were always female English names. Now the names alternate between male and female and are English, Spanish, and French.

Glossary

breeze—wind that blows gently

cluster—to group together

disturbances—an interruption

droplets—small drops of water or fluid

equator—the imaginary line around Earth halfway between the two poles

inland—an area away from a beach or waterfront

tropical—a warm, mild climate

vapor—steam or mist

To Learn More

At the Library

Berger, Melvin. *Hurricanes Have Eyes but Can't See*. New York: Scholastic, 2003.

Chambers, Catherine. *Hurricane*. Chicago: Heinemann Library, 2002.

Simon, Seymour. *Hurricanes*. New York: Morrow Junior Books, 1999.

On the Web

FactHound offers a safe, fun way to find Web sites related to this book. All of the sites on FactHound have been researched by our staff.

1. Visit *www.facthound.com*
2. Type in this special code: 1404809287
3. Click on the FETCH IT button.

Your trusty FactHound will fetch the best sites for you!

Index

Look for all of the books in this series:

Eye of the Storm: A Book About Hurricanes
Flakes and Flurries: A Book About Snow
Gusts and Gales: A Book About Wind
Nature's Fireworks: A Book About Lightning
Rising Waters: A Book About Floods
Rumble, Boom! A Book About Thunderstorms
Shapes in the Sky: A Book About Clouds
Sizzle! A Book About Heat Waves
Splish! Splash! A Book About Rain
Sunshine: A Book About Sunlight
Twisters: A Book About Tornadoes
Whiteout! A Book About Blizzards